I0484825

PAPARAZZI-FREE
PROPERTY SALE

PAPARAZZI-FREE PROPERTY SALE

TRAVIS JOHN
MIAMI

Information that was accurate as of the time of publication may become outdated by marketplace changes or conditions, new or revised laws, or other circumstances. Any slights against individuals, companies, or organizations are unintentional. All the examples in the book are based on assumptions no later in time than March 2015; thus, these assumptions are not guaranteed and may be subject to change. As with all assumptions and examples, results may vary based on a wide range of factors unique to each person's situation.

Back Cover Sources:
1. Brennan, Morgan. Stealth 'Off-Market' Home Sales On The Rise Among The Super-Wealthy. Forbes. February 15, 2013.
http://www.forbes.com/sites/morganbrennan/
2013/02/15/
stealth-home-sales-on-the-rise-among-the-super-wealthy/
2. Abkowitz, Alyssa. Psst. Wanna Buy A House? To keep identities secret, more buyers cloak their home purchases in LLCs and trusts. The Wall Street Journal. Oct. 25, 2012.
http://online.wsj.com/news/articles/

SB100008723963904436841045780668806778422280?
3. Beale, Lauren. Celebrities and the wealthy find ways to keep home sales secret. Los Angeles Times. October 16, 2012.
http://articles.latimes.com/2012/oct/16/business/la-fi-secret-home-sales-20121016
4. Caplin, Ian. Privacy law: Celebrities have a right to be left alone. NY Times. July 8, 2004.
http://www.nytimes.com/2004/07/08/opinion/08iht-edcaplin_ed3_.html

Travis John Agency, LLC
Address: 601 Brickell Ave, Ste. 700 Miami, FL 33131
(next to BB&T Bank)
Phone: (305) 600-5200
Web: https://travisjohn.com
Email: travis@travisjohn.com

VERSION 1

DEDICATION

To Princess Diana

Contents

INTRODUCTION

A Letter from Travis John, Creator of the Privacy Sale®

This book starts with an almost rhetorical question: *Do you believe that you have the right to privacy?*

I hesitated to ask that question—much less open the book with it—because of course you believe that you have the right to privacy. As a public figure, you've been bombarded by media outlets, gossip rags, and new-shounds who are trying to intrude into your personal life.

Indeed, you and your team of property brokers, estate managers, assistants, and attorneys have probably already gone to great lengths to protect your privacy.

But the cornerstone of my philosophy is that you have a right to take whatever legal measures you can to reclaim your privacy and keep intruders out of your personal life. At the same time, you have the right to make as much money as you can from the sale of your home and to keep this income discreet and ... well, private.

As you will learn in this book, regardless of whether you have paparazzi camping out in front of your property or are plagued by other and perhaps deeper privacy concerns, this book serves as a guide for personalizing a property sale based on your individual concerns—what I call a Privacy Sale®. Although this book includes numerous examples that are based on mainstream paparazzi concerns, the privacy problems are just as grave for high-net-worth individuals regardless of whether or not they battle camera-crazed paparazzi.

As a marketing expert and a real estate broker, I have designed the Privacy Sale process to be the blueprint for how to sell your real estate for top market value without compromising your privacy. This book enhances the actions you and your team have already taken to protect your privacy and provides a refreshing vehicle that allows you to sell your home for as much money as (and often more than) you would through traditional means, all the while avoiding the hassles that are thrust upon a public figure.

It is my goal to show you a new and better way to sell your real estate—a way that doesn't require reinventing the wheel.

Think of it like this: If you were selling a car, you would have a dozen or more different paths for making the sale, all of which could be equally effective. None of these methods would seem out of the ordinary or particularly unusual. All of them would represent equally acceptable paths to selling a car.

On the other hand, if you are in the market to sell a home, your options become more limited. Most people believe that listing a property on MLS[1] is the only way to sell a home. They even frown upon the alternate options to MLS commonly referred to as "off-market listings," "pocket listings," "silent listings," or "exclusive listings," as though these were somehow outside the boundaries of normal and accepted behavior.

But as you are about to learn, MLS can be downright dangerous for public figures, at its worst. Even at its best, it will likely degrade the value of a public figure's home. (In fact, a Privacy Sale begins with opting out of MLS.)

---

1. "MLS" stands for Multiple Listing Service. The examples in this book are based on the United States where approximately 900 separate MLS databases (that have mutual agreements to data share among one another) are collectively referred to as "MLS".

And this is why the current system begs a deeper look. How can you get more people—people who are better qualified[2]—to look at your property without broadcasting the details of your personal life to the masses? So with that in mind, let me ask you a question ...

<hr />

2. "qualified" refers solely to a prospective buyer's financial ability to purchase a property. The information gathered from a buyer is to ensure the seller's privacy concerns are honored.

2

DO YOU BELIEVE THAT YOU HAVE THE RIGHT TO PRIVACY?

This question sounds ridiculous to most people's ears. Their answer, like yours, is probably a resounding yes!

And I agree. Of course you have a right to privacy—or at least you *should* have the right to be left alone.

Legally, though, the answer is different. You have the right to privacy only if the details of your personal life aren't a matter of public interest. If the public takes interest in your personal life—whether or not you have voluntarily thrust yourself into the limelight—privacy laws are tossed by the wayside. Paparazzi can hide outside your window; snap pictures while holding a camera in your face; publish embarrassing photographs of you, your children, and your spouse; and then share the most intimate information with gossip rags and "news" outlets.

And regardless of whether your status as a public figure has reached the level of celebrity, the details of your private life could emerge in such a way that your business holdings could be affected. A divorce and the subsequent division of assets could throw a wrench in a business deal when shareholders, worried about the future of your company, dump your stock.

Now let's add another factor to the mix: People are wired for interconnectivity. Even decent, modest, and respectful people want to know the details of your personal life. They waste hours and hours of their own lives on social media sites, maniacally searching for details about near-strangers' lives. They share information as a means of feeling connected to a larger social network.

Of course, "share information" is a euphemism for "gossip," and according to the American Psychology Association, about 65 percent of people's conversations involve gossip.

Making matters worse, people's ability to share information is growing. Thanks to modern technology and the Internet, human beings create more information in two days than they did between the dawn of civilization and the year 2003.[1]

There's big money in making sure this information is readily available. More people read gossip rags than read the Bible. And in its heyday, one of these gossip rags, too offensive to mention by name, was the top-selling magazine, outranking Time, Sports Illustrated, and every single reputable magazine out there. Today, its circulation has dropped but only because modern culture has paved the way for more and more tabloids to find their way into supermarket checkout lanes, gas stations, and homes across the country.

If that isn't compelling enough to make public figures cringe, consider that in the United States of America, several thousand online entertainment and gossip websites are dedicated to celebrities and public figures, with more springing up daily; the top outlets make about $100,000 a month in advertising revenue alone, according to Experian Hitwise.

1. Kirkpatrick, Marshall. "Google CEO Schmidt: 'People Aren''t Ready for the Technology Revolution.'" ReadWrite. Aug. 4, 2010. http://readwrite.com/2010/08/04/google_ceo_schmidt_people_arent_ready_for_the_tech.

It bears noting that privacy laws are being enacted, but they are often insufficient. In 2013, for instance, California made some headway when it passed its child paparazzi law, which makes it a misdemeanor for paparazzi to attempt to photograph or video-tape a child in a harassing manner if the image is being taken because the child's parent is a celebrity or public official.

The new law "will give children, no matter who their parents are, protection from harassers who go to extremes to turn a buck."[2] It's very important to note that the new law targets the photographer's conduct, not the act of taking a photograph. So the law will reduce the number of cameras that are two feet away from your child's face, but it won't restrict the paparazzi from actually taking photos. They can still take photos; they just can't do it in a "harassing" manner. How will this be evidenced? If you have ever

2. California Law SB-606 Harassment: http://leginfo.legislature.ca.gov/faces/billNav-Client.xhtml?bill_id=201320140SB606

tried to catch someone trespassing, you know the challenges of catching someone in the act, particularly when that person's job involves hiding in your bushes or camping out in front of your house or hotel for 15 hours.

Because the gossip rags and newshounds pay big money for these photos, the paparazzi will find a way to snap photos of your children, which, I would argue, is harassing in and of itself.

So the truth is that, yes, you should have a right to privacy, but as long as there is big money to be made from the details of your public life, you are not going to be protected by the already ineffective privacy laws.

The onus for protecting your private life and the personal lives of your loved ones falls on you, your managers, and your team of advisors.

Consider what will happen if you do not take responsibility for protecting your private life.

Imagine, for instance, that you are selling your home, a yacht, a piece of artwork, a private jet, or an exotic car.

The number of traditional means of listing your for-sale items is great.

That is, the number is great if you are a traditional person.

Take, for instance, MLS. MLS is a listing of every single home being sold by real estate brokers in the United States of America. Unless specifically exempted from MLS, every home that is being sold will be listed.

For most people, MLS is the go-to method of getting the word out ... if you DON'T have specific reasons for being discreet. If you are selling a home that is comparable to a number of homes that are listed or have sold on MLS, then MLS is a terrific source for showcasing your property. Unless you have special circumstances, you would be foolish not to list your property alongside its competing properties.

But what if your situation is not normal? What if you want your home to be seen by the right people, not by the masses?

If you are a public figure or wealth-holder, MLS is probably the last place you want to list your home. About one-quarter of all wealth-holders are already turning their back on MLS, in part because of privacy concerns. You see, "MLS" stands for "Multiple Listing Service," but the truth is that the word "multiple" in this context is a bit of an understatement. The information and data that are broadcast through MLS come from approximately 900 databases of homes for sale and for rent. These databases are the source of listings for more than four million existing homes that are on the market at any given time.

When a listing enters an MLS, it is syndicated to hundreds of websites. Other platforms repurpose it manually or use software that scrapes the data from the web.

The data on MLS is the gold that defines the

value of the system. MLS can then sell this gold to other platforms, such as Zillow®, Trulia®, or Homes.com®.

And here is where the problem truly comes to light for public figures: Once a listing enters an MLS and the other accompanying platforms, the details of your home, yacht, car, or artwork become the property of these platforms.

This means the details of your address, the images of your child's bedroom, and the pictures of your bathroom have entered the public domain, as have the number of days your property has been on the market and whether the listing price has been reduced.

They can easily be shared with and accessed by media outlets. And this is only the tip of the iceberg.

Reflect on how easily this lack of discretion can invade not only your privacy but also your freedom. Your privacy allows you a few precious moments where you can be a distinct and separate individual. It is your gold. Yet too many people are trying to take this away from you. You don't need someone to tell you that if you are a public figure, the list of people who want to spread gossip about you is lengthy. So too is the list of people who will defame you, muddle up your property sale, derail your business deal, and spy on you and your family, with the intention of stealing from you or wreaking havoc on your life.

People can now visit your home. If you are living there, your children will be harassed as celebrity hounds pose as potential buyers or brokers who want to enter your home for a viewing. If you have already moved out, a number of additional security concerns come into play. How many people will try to break into your home just to snap a few pictures or for the mere thrill of setting foot in your home?

Guess what else is going to enter the picture? Speculators, who are going to wonder why you are selling your home. The questions will start buzzing: Are you unable to afford the home? Are you getting divorced? Was the home a bad investment? Are you losing money? Where are you going to move? Is something amiss in your personal life?

Oh, there's more! What does this say about your business holdings? Did your company take a turn for the worse? Should investors dump stock they hold in any of your business endeavors? Are you trying to raise money because you made a bad investment somewhere else?

From a privacy standpoint alone, using a traditional method of publicizing the sale of a piece of property is terrible. The seller's privacy is invaded, and even once the home is sold, the new buyer has almost no way of removing these images.

There's another consideration: All this publicity will hurt the value of your property.

When a public figure's home is for sale, photos of the home are published not only on traditional listing sites but also in magazines and on gossip blogs. Television shows will run stories about your home.

All this attention could cause a buyer whose interest in discretion matches yours to lose interest in a piece of property. With all the media scrutiny directed toward the home, high-end buyers could very well decide to steer clear, directing their attention toward properties that are being listed under the radar.

If you need to lower the asking price of the home, look out. This brings double trouble. Not only will you earn less on the sale, but media outlets also could raise conjectures about why you are unable to sell the home. You must be in a desperate financial crunch, they will guess. This property has been on the market for 387 days! They must be anxious to dump it, the media will say, "sharing information" that may or may not be true with potential buyers.

One way or another, though, the price of your home will drop.

Even if you are a public figure—in fact, especially if you are a public figure—you have the right to protect the details of your own life, protect the value of your home, and protect the life of your family members when you decide to sell your property. You have the right to keep your child's address out of the public eye, and you have the right to seek top market value for your home.

And yet the current privacy laws are not doing nearly enough to protect you or your family members. In fact, almost anyone can become a "public figure," thereby excluding him or her from the limited protection a person does have from slander and defamation. In turn, the value of your home is not protected.

Unfortunately, you and your managers are solely responsible for taking action to protect yourself, your assets, and the people you love most.

And this is just one of the reasons why so many public figures are turning their backs on MLS. At the peak of its popularity just a few years ago, anywhere from 80 to 90 percent of all sales in any given local market were facilitated or generated through a broker using MLS. Today, that has changed, particularly in high-value areas and hot markets. In California, Florida, and New York, for instance, as many as one out of four homes for sale is not listed on MLS, and in other affluent neighborhoods, as many as 33 percent of homes are sold without using MLS.

These sales are often defined as "exclusivity," "off market," or "pocket listing" sales. Whatever someone calls these sales, the inherent concern of people who are selling their homes without listing on MLS is this: *How can I market my home, sell it at top value, and still have my privacy?* You can't post a sign in your yard or an ad on Craigslist. And word of mouth will go only so far.

Fortunately, there is a better way—one that

allows public figures to protect their privacy when selling real estate while still showing the home to qualified buyers. *The Paparazzi-Free Property Sale* will share the Privacy Sale® process with you that will make the entire process private. You will have complete control over who knows and, perhaps more important, who doesn't know about the sale of your property.

This book provides an alternative to the normal process of selling property. It excludes the property from MLS (and other traditional listing sites) while still providing a laser-focused marketing plan so that you can attract a buyer who will purchase your home for top market price.

A Privacy Sale is a little like an off-market listing ... on steroids. You see, a Privacy Sale has aggregated all of the best off-market practices into one solution that protects your privacy. A Privacy Sale doesn't restrict how much money you will make on your home sale, and it causes you far fewer headaches. It is my goal for a Privacy Sale to be an accepted standard. For nontraditional sellers, I don't want MLS to be the golden rule. Instead, all sellers and buyers can have an open and free market to buy and sell their most valuable assets as they choose.

At the core of the Privacy Sale is the idea that the flow of personal information should be targeted, directed, and discreet. Popular opinion holds that under a free society, public information must flow freely. While that might be true, it is also true that personal information should be under the direct control of the individual. Without control over our private lives, we lose our own individual freedom.

And this is why a Privacy Sale is being introduced as a new and improved way of selling real estate.

In fact, a Privacy Sale has 10 components to protect your interests—namely, your privacy and your home's selling price. These components are called the 10 P's, and in one fashion or another, they frame the entire Privacy Sale process. I designed the 10 P's with the goal of giving you at least 10 times the privacy you would normally have when selling your home through traditional methods.

This book is dedicated to describing these 10 P's in detail so that you, your broker [34],your attorney, and your team of advisors can decide whether the Privacy Sale process will meet your unique goals.

For now, here is a brief review of the 10 P's.

The 10 Components of the Privacy Sale Process

1. A Privacy Sale is **personalized** to you. In the pursuit of privacy, you might have specific concerns about the details of your privacy. Because a Privacy Sale is fully customized, a

---

3. For the purpose of this book, it is assumed that you are using a real estate broker to represent you. This broker will follow these 10 P's when selling your real estate.

4. Herein, the word "broker" is used to describe a licensed real estate professional; "broker" can mean the same thing as "agent."

broker will take these concerns into consideration before considering a broader marketing plan.

2. A broker will spend a tremendous amount of time **preparing** for the sale of your home. This will start by opting out of MLS. Then, after your services are personalized, a broker will use kid gloves to make sure the marketing initiative is established to protect you while still getting the best exposure for your property. For example, a broker will use a password-protected portal that will allow potential buyers to view specific details of your home while still protecting the flow of information.

3. A broker will consider how to **position** your property so that you have the most success. A broker will consider all of the ways to position and place your property for sale so that the right buyer will be attracted to your property. Brokers focus on creating a consistent story around your property that is specific to the target audience that has been

identified. Then the message is tailored to appeal to each audience.

4. A broker will promote your property by using the **people power** of direct marketing. Brokers should have a large network of partners (real estate managers, assistants, other brokers, and the like) and a list of qualified high-end buyers who would be interested in a home similar to yours. This powerful network is a gold mine. It bridges together the right people at the right time.

5. A broker will **promote** your property using a personalized plan. This might include advertisements on targeted industry websites and in publications. Of course, a broker will always build these promotions on a foundation of privacy. When a broker promotes your home, all identifying information will always be scrubbed from the public eye.

6. A broker will use aggressive **private relationship** tactics to build a database of buyers. Private relations is like public relations but without the disclosure of any information

about your home. By using direct marketing to showcase their accomplishments and reputation in the media, prospective buyers are more inclined to register with the network so that they can see the most exclusive off-market listings.

7. A broker will make **personal appearances** at industry association meetings, always keeping his or her ears open for estate managers, assistants, and brokers who represent clients who are looking to buy real estate. Your broker will have one-on-one meetings with his or her affiliates and strategic partners during the sale of your real estate.

8. A broker will honor the **prosperity** path. This is the "Yellow Brick Road" the broker will use to monitor the success of the marketing plan for your property. Your broker should be dedicated to exceeding your expectations for success, profitability, ease, comfort, and security by carefully monitoring all activities and outcomes associated with your home.

9. Sellers are encouraged to **protect** themselves by working with their attorneys to ensure the proper legal and asset protection mechanisms are in place and so that your privacy is maintained.

10. And finally, your privacy will be **preserved**. Not only will everyone involved accept the terms of mutual confidentiality and nondisclosure, but the broker will also make sure that every partner respects your need for privacy. This will begin with your broker not recording your sale on MLS, even after it is completed. And no one will exploit your celebrity status, nor will your broker glorify his or her services by leveraging the power of your name.

3

WHAT IS A PRIVACY SALE®?

"Whenever you find your self on the side of the majority, it is time to pause and reflect." – Mark Twain

A Privacy Sale is a unique process for public figures (celebrities, high-profile business leaders, politicians, and other public figures and wealth-holders) to keep their real estate (usually in excess of $5 million dollars) "off market" while still selling it at top market value.

Using a technology solution combined with a personalized, private, yet aggressive marketing funnel, a broker will bridge together other high-end brokers, buyers, and sellers, using mutual confidentiality and nondisclosure agreements to protect both the seller and the buyer.

A Privacy Sale can be compared to how a family office operates or even the private banking model that arose out of wealth holders wanting to have more privacy, confidentiality and personalized services.

In its simplest form, a Privacy Sale is a discreet marketing endeavor. It neither replaces the need for a seller to hire a broker nor requires reinventing the wheel. The seller's broker will follow a Privacy Sale process as a means of maximizing exposure to the property because it provides a private yet power-ful way to find affluent buyers. One of the ways the broker accomplishes this is by designing a small and intimate private net-work. This network allows top brokers to pri-vately connect and conduct business by matching their high-end buyers with their most exclusive off-market listings. As in a traditional transaction, the seller pays the real estate commission that is agreed upon with the listing broker. And if a buyer is located by a cooperating broker[1], then that broker is paid out of the buyer's side of the advertised real estate commission.

Under a Privacy Sale, all the people who "sit at the table" will be fully vetted so that only qualified and interested buyers will see your home. Though the broker wants to aggres-sively build the largest pool of potential buy-ers for your property, a broker also realizes that you would much rather market to the

[1]. "cooperating broker" is the broker who locates a buyer for the property and represents the buyer's interests during negotiation (while the listing broker represents the seller).

700 people who can actually buy your property than to the millions of people who can access an MLS website.

So instead of saying, "Look at me!" a Privacy Sale asks, "Are you qualified to look at me?" When less than 1 percent of the population can afford to buy your property, there is no reason why it should be brokered to the masses.

Under a Privacy Sale:

- The address of your home will never be listed in a public domain.
- Images and details about the property will be used sparingly in the public domain.
- Your name will never be used to market your home.
- No buyer will ever contact you directly.
- There will be no record of any price changes or of the number of days your home has been on the market.
- You and your broker can track

which potential buyers have shown an interest in your home.

Because of this, you will be better positioned to stay in control of the sale of your home. Instead of letting external factors take control of a potential buyer's thought process, both buyer and seller will focus on the transaction only.

Although the number of people who see your listing will be greatly reduced, the number of qualified buyers who view your listing will actually increase. By controlling the flow of information, the broker gets the right information in the hands of all the people who might want to buy your home, whether they live five miles away or 5,000 miles away.

A broker's network consists of other top brokers, estate managers, publicists, assistants, attorneys, and high-end buyers around the world. Instead of using a massive system that is broken, a broker connects the people who are most likely to buy your home by providing them with buyer-relevant listings.

A broker's goal is not to simply restrict the flow of your property information but also to:

1. Maintain the highest quality and integrity by directing the flow of your property details appropriately.

2. Provide you with ultimate control of the flow of information surrounding your private life.

A broker provides a buying and selling environment that connects your property to the right audience. The goal of a Privacy Sale is to provide an exclusive network for you to sell your property for the highest possible price, with the best terms that can be negotiated, in the most expedient manner, and with the least amount of hassle to you and your family.

So What Does a Typical Privacy Sale Look Like?

It bears noting that there is no "typical" Privacy Sale. Just as with any marketing initiative, each Privacy Sale is customized to protect the seller's unique needs and to best position the home. With that said, the following is a general idea of the Privacy Sale process.

The Privacy Sale process has three components: 1) the quality of the broker's network, 2) the broker's process for protecting your privacy and the flow of your property's information, and 3) the personalized marketing plan.

Let's start by taking a look at the quality of the broker's network. I have a saying about the importance of your broker's network: *A broker's network affects your net worth.* For this reason, a broker will stack his or her network with:

Qualified buyers. A great broker has a pre-existing network of qualified and vetted buyers. Before receiving detailed information about a piece of real estate, a buyer should agree to the confidentiality and nondisclosure terms and provide the broker with a pre-qualification letter or proof of funds. The privacy in a Privacy Sale is a two-way street, which protects the buyer's privacy as well.

Brokers are constantly building and refining their list of buyers. They use direct marketing to reach out to people who fit the profile of a likely buyer. They advertise their firm in magazines that are widely read by high-networth people who could be buyers for your property. They join and become active participants in organizations for domestic estate managers, celebrity assistants, real estate attorneys, financial planners, estate attorneys, real estate brokers, and the like.

Speaking of other brokers, real estate attorneys and financial planners, a broker's network includes **strategic partners**, who are other professionals and vendors who have a degree of intimacy with high-net-worth people.

Arguably the most important component of a strong network is the broker's relationship with other **accomplished brokers.** By nurturing relationships, other top brokers can discreetly match their qualified buyers with your one-of-a-kind property.

The quality of this network is critical to the success of a Privacy Sale. In the end, it's a broker's exhaustive marketing efforts and tight-knit relationships that allows them to connect with affluent buyers—who also crave off-market property and the privacy they bring.

In addition to a network that allows a broker access to high-net-worth buyers around the world, a broker will also have a secure portal, which provides a bridge between the seller's property listing and the buyer. This is a marketing platform where a buyer can view and connect with the most exclusive off-market listings.

Keep in mind that each property portal is accessible to registered buyers and brokers only.

Remember that the broker's portal:

- Will never list your address without your permission.
- Does not provide the buyer with any method of contacting you directly.
- Does not list any price changes or the number of days your home has been on the market.

In general, the process works like this:

- A seller lists his or her property exclusively with the broker by entering into the seller-broker agreement. This is nothing new, and it represents the beginning of almost every seller's plan.
- The details of the property—including photographs and the floor plan but not the owner's name (or address, unless the owner gives permission) or other identifying information—are hosted

on a secure and confidential property portal so they can be conveniently viewed by qualified, and approved brokers and buyers.

- A link to the listing on the members-only portal is sent to a qualified database of buyers who match the specification of the property and the requirements of the buyer.
- The same link is sent to all of the brokers in the network, who canvass their database to identify suitable and qualified buyers.
- Suitable buyers make arrangements with their broker to inspect the property at convenient times.
- Negotiations take place through the real estate broker, the seller, and the buyer.

Your broker will monitor all buyers' activities, keeping tabs on which potential buyers have inquired about your home.

The broker's network and his or her portal work hand in hand. When a new property portal is created, for instance, a broker will alert all of his or her broker partners via email, letting them know that a new property has been listed and that they should enter the secure portal for more information.

The third part of finding the right buyer for your home is to create a personalized marketing plan. This plan is directly influenced by the seller's specific needs. One seller might want to list photos of the home (without an address or other identifying information) on websites and in publications that are read by high-net-worth individuals. Another seller might be reticent to have any information enter the public domain, regardless of whether the details have been scrubbed. For this seller, the broker might create a direct marketing plan where he or she sends personalized letters (with or without pictures) to individual buyers, letting them know some of the highlights of the home.

This is the big-picture view of the Privacy Sale process, which concludes with a buyer finding a home, at which point the buyer's and seller's attorneys usually enter the picture to make sure that the property is transferred into a trust or another mechanism (such as an LLC owned by a trust) that protects the buyer's privacy as well.

Section 4 goes into much greater detail about the keys to success of a Privacy Sale.

4

THE SUCCESS OF A PRIVACY SALE®

～∽～

Section 3 took a big-picture look at what a broker will do to help you sell your property for the most amount of money while still protecting your privacy and creating the least amount of hassle for you and your family. Section 4 goes deeper so that owners of high-end property know exactly how to have success with a Privacy Sale.

The success of a Privacy Sale is contingent on three key factors:

- Finding the right broker for your needs,
- The broker's private network, and
- The personalized marketing plan.

Let's take a look at these one at a time.

The first key is to make sure you have the right broker representing your best interests. Below I provide the six key factors that I believe can be used to help determine whether you have the right match for your needs. It is my belief that a broker has to be more than qualified; a broker must be the right broker for you.

The Broker-Matching Process

1. First comes the broker's **personal character**. Without a doubt, the broker has a fiduciary duty to you. They should also have integrity

and be trustworthy and dependable. A broker is expected to demonstrate these character traits in every contact with you, your family, and all other professionals and buyers with whom the broker will communicate.

2. The broker's **personality**. Selling a valuable piece of property requires a certain level of intimacy, so you should seek to work with brokers with whom you can develop rapport. To make the process as smooth as possible, the broker and you must see eye to eye on important issues. You and the broker should have the right chemistry. He or she needs to be a great listener and a tough negotiator.

3. The broker's **passion** is a critical component of a Privacy Sale. The broker must be truly concerned about you and your family and should understand what is most critical to you, beginning with the property sale objectives. Brokers should care more about you and your family than they do about making a sale.

4. Brokers are exceptionally **proficient**. Bro-

kers constantly demonstrate that they are exceptional at managing all the aspects of a property sale. The broker should have implemented key best practices for serving you, including systems for identifying and systematically addressing your most important real estate and privacy concerns.

5. Brokers are top **producers**. Although several criteria determine why brokers are the best in the business, one way you can determine this is by evaluating an individual broker's sales production. For example, he or she may have a sales volume of at least $10 million annually.

6. A broker is your **partner**. The relationship you have with your broker frames the entire sales process. You should know that your broker is in communication with you, closely working with you to identify your key goals, values, and issues and creating and implementing plans for systematically addressing them all. This is crucial during your sale, but

the right partner is one who can also be counted on for exceptional after-sale service.

By following this matching process, you will have the greatest chance of working with a broker who has the ability to meet your unique needs, desires, pressures, and lifestyle.

The second key is for a broker to maintain his or her own private network that will discreetly connect one-of-a-kind properties with one-of-a-kind buyers. This starts with being connected to the right brokers who represent affluent sellers and buyers like *you*.

To become a part of a broker's private network, other brokers should go through a vetting process to join the network. In its simplest form, the network can be best described as brokers with exclusive lists of unique properties that *won't be found in the public domain or on an MLS*. Other high-end real estate brokers want to be included in this network because it provides them access to the most exclusive and luxurious listings in their community, usually in excess of $5 million dollars, that are not being marketed through traditional methods. In addition, it provides a way for the brokers representing sellers to notify members of the network of their exclusive off-market listings and find a buyer.

A broker's network becomes a marketing platform that can deliver huge results. Not only do brokers market your property using a private portal, but they also use their marketing muscles to implement direct marketing and advertising plans that increase exposure to all of their exclusive property listings. This results in more buyer inquiries and more visibility on the local, national, and international levels.

In other words, the broker's private network provides a back door to connect the most accomplished luxury real estate brokers, buyers, and partners in his or her community. It's a network filled with people who are plugged into current trends, keeping each other abreast of current best practices. Because the integrity of the network depends on the quality of each of its players, these high-end professionals share knowledge and work with each other so that the entire network stays ahead of the curve. This means that sellers who work with a broker can leverage a treasure trove of cutting-edge marketing and sales strategies so that your home is targeted to a qualified audience of influential home buyers, affluent investors, renowned business leaders, celebrated industry professionals, and other qualified persons of interest.

Many of these buyers and professionals would otherwise be inaccessible, as they have their own privacy gates as well. Others are in foreign countries, such as the United Kingdom, China, Brazil, Canada, Japan, and India. By working within the private network, sellers and their brokers can find these buyers and connect with local professionals who speak the language and understand cultural etiquette, giving a seller's broker access to the resources he or she needs to handle high-end (and therefore sensitive) transactions. In other words, these brokers have a local footprint and a global reach.

A broker's private network is the Four Seasons for real estate professionals, so you will always know that your broker has a concierge for all the top people, buyers, and business connections. Only the most accomplished real estate brokers in a community are invited to join a private network. Then the brokers must complete a vetting process to be accepted into the network. Although the vetting process is thorough, it should also be efficient and timely. By making it a fast but efficient process, brokers (and buyers) don't lose interest in joining the network, and the network quality is never sacrificed.

Here are the suggested requirements a broker would complete electronically before being accepted into the private network:

- Complete a broker profile.

- Provide references and successes.
- Agree to a code of ethics, mutual nondisclosure and confidentiality terms.

Once it is determined that the broker is a leader in his or her field, exceeds the network's service standards, and demonstrates a proven record of success, the broker is accepted into the network.

For added quality assurance, the broker should provide ongoing due diligence of the other brokers' status and performance.

The third key of the Privacy Sale process is the broker's ability to execute an effective and discreet marketing plan.

Execution of a Privacy Sale is largely dependent upon the marketing plan and resources used by the broker. Brokers design a targeted marketing plan that maximizes response and buyer interest in the property.

This includes the following:

- A broker uses professional copywriting services so that all communications with buyers include psychological triggers that encourage buyer interest in a property.
- A broker places ads in publications that are read by high-net-worth individuals, but unless the ad is results driven and visually stunning, it will be for naught. Therefore, brokers will buy and prepare only results-driven ad copy.
- A broker will advertise the property on leading luxury home websites that allow for the property address to be hidden.
- A broker emphasizes strategy over tactics. Marketing tactics are usually commonplace, but knowing how to effectively implement, test, trigger, and modify the tactics determines their success.
- When appropriate, a broker will send professionally written direct

mail to targeted lists of public figures and/or their managers.

- Through magazine ads and value-added giveaways, brokers drive web traffic to single-purpose websites to convert traffic into potential buyers.
- Because most buyers will not be immediately ready to buy, brokers use a system to continue nurturing the potential buyers in the network. This "touch strategy" allows buyers to be kept abreast of current and relevant information through free reports, resource guides, emails, and other products so that these buyers remain engaged up through the time they decide to buy.

Remember, brokers work within the framework of the 10 P's so that the seller's privacy is maintained while an "underground" marketing initiative allows the buyer's property to be seen by as many potential buyers as possible. Following the 10 P's is critical to the success of the marketing plan. Although this is not an exhaustive list, the remainder of this section is dedicated to explaining the 10 P's in detail and how they are crucial to the success of a marketing plan.

1. Because no two clients and no two properties are exactly alike, a Privacy Sale is **personalized** to you—the seller. A broker performs a free Privacy Sale audit to discuss specific concerns of your privacy, making sure these concerns are respected while creating a marketing plan. For instance, some sellers are willing to disclose the home's address to vetted buyers. Others are more comfortable giving the buyers a general idea of the location, but the exact address is not disclosed until a buyer expresses a high level of interest in the property. Information like this is gathered during the Privacy Sale audit.

2. A broker will spend a tremendous amount of time preparing for the sale of your home.

This includes:

- Creating a story

- Creating a marketing plan

The Story

Most brokers focus primarily on the facts and features of the home when they advertise it to the market. Through digital brochures, print marketing, web marketing, video tours, and the like, a broker focuses on telling the story of your home and its special benefits. The difference is subtle but powerful. You see, buyers will care about the facts and features of your home only if they care about your home. They must first make an emotional connection, which a broker creates by forging a connection between the home and the story.

This story usually includes what I call the "Secret Treasure" component. I know that high-end buyers are attracted to the idea of finding a gem that is not officially "on the market." The broker's private network, therefore, is known as the resource for finding hidden treasures that no one knows about.

The Marketing Plan

Marketing plans vary in costs from property to property but can cost a broker up to 1 percent of a home's selling price. As part of the process of preparing a home, a broker will set up a password-protected portal for the property. Details of the property – including high-quality professional photographs, a full-color professional brochure, and a visually rich property tour—are hosted on this secure and confidential portal so they can be conveniently viewed online.

The details of the property are then sent to a qualified database of buyers who match the specifications of the property and requirements of the buyers. These are emailed and/or sent via direct mail. The link to the property is also sent to preferred brokers who canvass their database to identify suitable buyers who are qualified. Your property's information, therefore, circulates only among a connected and vetted network of brokers and their high-end clientele. A well-connected broker, therefore, is the determining factor of these deals.

All online and offline media promotions will lead back to this page, which offers more information about the home.

Depending on the personalized plan, some brokers will send password-protected email communications and/or PDF file attachments to interested buyers. Others will provide a phone number so that interested buyers can call and listen to a recorded message that tells the story about the property and directs the buyer to become registered in the broker's system.

3. The broker considers how to **position** your property so that you have the most success. This means that the broker considers how to place your property for sale so that the right buyer is attracted to your property. This is where brokers begin to flex their marketing muscles. In the fifth of the 10 P's (promote), I mention many tools a broker will use, such as a launching plan, videos, direct mail, free

reports, referral programs, online events, retargeting ads, and the like. It bears noting, though, that not every tool is successful for marketing every home. By planning, positioning, testing, and tweaking promotions for the property and using the appropriate tools, the plan gets the best exposure to yield the highest price.

4. A broker will promote your property using the **people power** of direct marketing. Brokers have a large network of strategic partners and alliances that already have relationships with potential buyers.

These partners and alliances include:

- Accountants
- Other brokers, including real estate, yacht, and mortgage brokers
- Attorneys
- Financial advisors
- Life insurance agents
- Property and casualty agents
- Association executives
- Business brokers

- Investment bankers
- Personal assistants and gatekeepers
- Yacht captains
- Members of executive concierge services
- Members of exclusive clubs
- Agents for public figures
- Private lenders of super jumbo mortgage loans
- Publicists
- Estate and household managers
- Custom home builders

Brokers also have a list of qualified and prominent buyers who would be interested in a home similar to yours. This powerful network is a gold mine. It bridges together the right people at the right time.

Because the network of a broker affects your net worth, a top broker will stack his or her network with the right strategic partners to privately yet aggressively market your home through word of mouth.

All of these people connect through a private

portal that allows the broker to communicate through private messages to network members with details about the property listing so that qualified buyers can be identified.

5. A broker will **promote** your property using your personalized plan. Following is a list of tools, platforms, and tactics a broker might use to market a home. Once again, this is not an exhaustive list, as the specific tools would be contingent upon a person's personalized marketing plan.

Email marketing: A broker will notify his or her database of vetted buyers and brokers that your property has been added to the private portal.

Advertisements and media buying: A broker would advertise on online and offline media outlets that are viewed by high-net-worth individuals, such as major and niche websites, magazines, journals, newspapers, mobile apps, radio and television. These ads would direct the viewer to a single purpose website of your property and/or to call a dedicated phone number for more information.

Websites: A broker would direct media ads to single purpose websites that feature your property but hide your property address and limit details that can be viewed publicly. These websites exist to encourage prospective buyers to request more information about your property. These websites often include value-added freebies (such as free reports, resource guides, podcasts, online events, or privacy audits) that are given away in exchange for a person's name and email address. This allows a broker to find (and then vet) more potential buyers for your property.

Direct response mail: A broker would implement an expertly crafted direct mail campaign to reach a very specific list of prospective buyers. This starts by sending targeted mail to their own list of prospects and to other top brokers not yet in their network that represent buyers looking for similar properties. The broker will further expand their reach by identifying third-party mailing lists of prospective buyers. For instance, wealth-holders that already own property at or near a beach or ones that are equestrian enthusiasts. These lists are either bought or rented from targeted media sources that provide information or services specifically to high-net-worth individuals. For example, a broker would be better served by buying a list of subscribers to *Forbes* Newsletters than to *Forbes* magazine, as the former has a higher-net-worth client list. A broker could then send letters, greeting cards, postcards, or "lumpy mail," meaning mail that obviously has something inside other than a letter. This is called a "grabber," and it might be a small bag of beach sand to symbolize the beach lifestyle that accompanies the unique home that is described in the enclosed letter. This grabber is intended to pique the interest of the recipient and ties into the special benefits of the home that is being offered for sale. Critical to the success of a direct response mail campaign is that a professional copywriter writes the mail. For a piece of mail to be considered "direct response," the mail must 1) have an offer, 2) include a reason that compels the recipient to respond immediately, and 3) include a code or phone number that allows the mail to be tracked.

Display ads and pay-per-click: A broker might buy ads on major and niche websites. For example, a broker can advertise the home on a local luxury website that caters to affluent buyers in the surrounding area. Or, promote the home on a national or multinational website that focuses on a particular lifestyle that the property affords. Another option for the broker is to promote the home on social media websites like Facebook or LinkedIn. Although these sites have a broad reach, their advanced advertising platforms allow the broker to be very selective of who can see their ads. The broker accomplishes this by selecting a Facebook or LinkedIn custom audience, list or group that meets a specific set of criteria. Of course, the ads are scrubbed of identifying material.

Retargeting: Brokers can use something called "retargeting" or "remarketing" to show the ads to users who have previously visited a website. Imagine that a potential buyer visits the single-purpose landing page but does not provide his or her name or email address. The computer browser will recognize that the person had at least a bit of interest in the home, and it will later retarget by showing another ad promoting the same home, perhaps while the person is logged onto Facebook.

Codes: So that the marketing plan can be evaluated and modified, when necessary, a broker uses trackable phone numbers and URLs to keep track of which advertising is working and which advertising is not drawing attention.

Proprietary books, magazines, and ebooks: Some brokers even create their own magazines, ebooks, and hard-copy books that are targeted to high-net-worth individuals.

6. Brokers use aggressive **private relationship**

tactics to build their database of buyers. Private relations is like public relations but without the disclosure of any information about your home. Brokers use digital marketing and interactive public relations, such as search engine ranking, to build their name and reputation. They also participate in publicity events and speaking opportunities and write press releases, newsletters, blogs, podcasts, and outbound communications. Brokers can write for industry magazines to grow their own exposure, thereby encouraging potential buyers to join their network. By using direct marketing to showcase their accomplishments and reputation in the media, prospective buyers are more inclined to register with the network so that they can see the most exclusive off-market listings.

A broker will make **personal appearances** at association meetings, trade shows, seminars, charity events, and networking groups attended by potential buyers and/or their representatives, always keeping his or her ears open for estate managers, assistants, brokers, and clients who are looking to buy real estate. Your broker will have one-on-one meetings with his or her strategic partners during the sale of your real estate.

Your broker will honor the **prosperity path**. This is the "Yellow Brick Road" the broker will use to monitor the success of the marketing plan and the efficacy of ads for your property by tracking the buyers who are viewing your home via the portal. Your broker should be dedicated to exceeding your expectations for success, profitability, ease, comfort, and security by delivering a dream-come-true experience for you.

Sellers are encouraged to **protect** themselves. A broker not only vets buyers, brokers, and partners before bringing anyone to the table, but he or she also encourages both buyers and sellers to protect their privacy by working with their attorneys to establish the proper trust mechanisms (or LLCs owned by trusts) so that everyone's privacy is maintained once the home has been sold.

Along the way, the broker requires a buyer to provide proof of funds, to agree to the confidentiality and nondisclosure terms, and to view the home only after being qualified. The secure portal is also guided by this principle of protection—the portal can restrict the downloading of photos, floor plans, or brochures, all of which can be tastefully watermarked to discourage dissemination.

The final P is **preservation,** meaning that your privacy is **preserved before, during, and after the sale.** Not only does everyone involved accept mutual confidentiality and nondisclosure terms, but the system also makes sure that every partner will respect your need for privacy. A broker realizes that if his or her network's integrity is compromised, the service is no longer valuable. This means that the broker will not use your status as a public figure for his or her gain unless you have explicitly granted this by way of an endorsement or testimonial. In short, your privacy is honored, and every single person invited to the table will honor your privacy in perpetuity.

5

CONCLUSION

———— ༄ ————

> "Privacy is not something that I'm merely entitled to, it's an absolute prerequisite." – Marlon Brando

You should be able to sell your property and be left alone.

It is that simple and that obvious. Unfortunately, it isn't that easy. If you are a public figure, a wide range of people are interested in the most intimate details of your life. Some of them will lie, cheat, and steal so that they can violate your privacy.

The Privacy Sale process offers a new and better way to fend off those privacy violators and market your property only to the people who should see your message. By providing a marketing platform and a vetted network of quality buyers and their brokers, your broker can exchange the open front door that allows the world to invade your privacy for a 24/7 guard gate.

Think of a Privacy Sale as an exclusive club for public figures and their representatives. Instead of using the traditional one-size-fits-all property sale model, you have a discreet and custom-tailored property sale that commands the best terms that can be negotiated, in the most expedient manner, and with the least amount of hassle to you and your family.

If you are a public figure selling a property, a Privacy Sale is your best choice because it allows you:

- Protection
- Autonomy
- A financial advantage

Let's take a look at these one at a time.

A Privacy Sale protects you and your family.

Vandalism, break-ins, harm to your family members, public defamation: These are all outcomes of a market listing. If you are living in the home, you and your family could be harassed. If you aren't living in the home, your valuables (and the home itself) could be at risk.

And you face a variety of nuisances if your home is listed publicly, not the least of which is intentional interference with your legal right to prospective economic advantage. Beyond that, your reputation could be damaged if the public begins speculating as to why you are selling your home.

In the end, a market listing harms you and the eventual sale price of your home, whereas a Privacy Sale protects you, your family, your reputation, your belongings, and the sale price of your home.

Beyond that, your home is a sacred space. It is where you have freedom to live your life without the interference of paparazzi, investors, reporters, and the general public. If your home is listed through a traditional MLS, this sanctuary could be trespassed upon by any number of people. A Privacy Sale recognizes how sacred a home is, and it protects your right to privacy while still earning you top market value.

A Privacy Sale gives you autonomy.

You deserve to be in control of your personal life, maintain your freedom, and be empowered to make sound business decisions about your property sale. A Privacy Sale makes sense for several reasons, most of which are related to positive events, such as selling a property to buy a bigger one, cashing in on a great investment, or getting married. However, other circumstances that lead to the sale of a home include financial troubles, divorce, short sale, or probate. One way or another, returning to normal life is impossible if you have to worry about what your neighbors think, what your critics think, what your friends think, and what the public thinks.

A Privacy Sale removes all of the outside voices and allows you to be in control of your own thoughts and your own decisions.

A Privacy Sale gives you a financial advantage.

A property that is listed on an MLS ages like stale bread. It starts by being marketed to an audience that is too broad. Then not only will the media report about the property sale, so too will bloggers and gossip rags. All of this overexposure will saturate the market and drive the price down as your potential buyers, who probably also crave privacy, begin looking for properties that offer a little more discretion.

And if the price does go down, you very well

might be on a slippery slope. When the public learns that you have lowered the property's price tag, speculators will begin questioning your financial stability, the health of your investments, and the implications these will have for your future.

Because a Privacy Sale occurs behind closed doors, you are able to send the right message to the right audience without having the home's price commanded by irrelevant external factors. You and your buyer are able to negotiate fairly, which means the true market value of your home will be honored.

Get started with a Privacy Sale.

This book provides a suggested outline of what you can do to follow the Privacy Sale process. If you believe that a Privacy Sale is right for you, I encourage you to share this book with your broker and team of advisors. Remember, you don't have to reinvent the wheel. The Privacy Sale process simply enhances your broker's services by combining the right people and the right systems to solve your need, which is selling your home at top market value while protecting your privacy.

Consider a second opinion.

You already have a relationship with a real estate broker. You may even work with several brokers. If you are completely satisfied with these relationships and confident that your real estate affairs are on the right track, great! But if you wonder whether another broker is better suited to address your family's very specific Privacy Sale and real estate goals, you're not alone. Successful people are successful because they always seek out the highest-quality advisors.

By getting a second opinion, you can verify two things: 1) whether you have a broker who understands your unique needs, desires, pressures and lifestyle; and 2) whether your quality of service could be improved.

I appreciate your taking the time to read this

book, and I look forward to hearing about your success.

P.S. If you'd like some help with a Privacy Sale, let's talk. I'll set aside time to talk personally with you or someone from your team of advisors.

When you schedule an exploratory call with me, I can help you determine whether your quality of service could be improved. After I listen and understand your unique needs, desires, pressures and lifestyle, I will create a comprehensive Privacy Sale plan based on all aspects of your privacy and related property sale goals. I will also give you my recommendations for addressing any concerns that need to be addressed.

NO, this call is not fluff...

On this call I'll help you come up with a strategic marketing plan for your Privacy Sale that your broker and team of advisors can implement on your behalf. Yes, if you like the plan we discuss, I encourage you to implement it yourself.

But if you see value in the plan and would like to initiate the broker second-opinion service, that's great too! You can just ask me to help you.

In that case, I will introduce you to a broker who has been carefully selected based on the qualification process described in this book. This broker will then meet with you and provide you with a second opinion.

My mission is to help public figures and their families make better-informed real estate decisions. One of the ways I reach this goal is by connecting you with a broker in your community. Through this second-opinion service, you will be able to quickly determine whether this broker is the right choice for you and your family.

No, this is not a sales pitch in disguise.

There is no charge and no obligation to use

this service. If you decide to do business with the broker you are referred to and that person is successful in selling your property, I may receive a referral fee from the broker. That's it.

I know that your time is valuable, and I have no intention of wasting it. In fact, the professionals in my network are focused only on attracting people who are serious about time, money and the sale of their home. The network becomes stronger only when the right people join, which is why brokers will not provide the second-opinion service unless they know they can help you.

Please visit www.privacysale.com/call to schedule a convenient time for an exploratory call with me.

Prior to our call, I will sign and send you a confidentiality and nondisclosure agreement. If you prefer to have your attorney draft the agreement, please be prepared to send this prior to our call.

Frequently
Asked
Questions

"Does your service help buyers? If so, can the Privacy Sale process work for me?"

Yes! Although this book was written with the privacy of sellers in mind, the process is successful ONLY when it connects a seller's property with the RIGHT buyer. Because a Privacy Sale requires a perfect balance of affluent buyers and sellers, a well-connected broker is equally committed to discreet and intimate relationships with prospective buyers.

Let's face it: you don't need a broker to tell you what properties are for sale on the open market—any website can tell you that information. But there are several value-driven reasons for an affluent buyer to seek out representation from a well-connected broker. The first and most obvious reason is that the broker will ensure you get access to any off-market properties for sale.

But it doesn't stop there. Well-connected brokers will proactively reach out to their network, other brokers and property owners to seek out properties that meet a buyer's criteria. The broker will make an exhaustive effort to locate these one-of-a-kind properties, and then notify the prospective sellers or their representatives that he has a client interested in buying a property similar to theirs. Finally, the broker will use his marketing muscle and relationship mojo to encourage these prospects to notify him if they would consider a sale.

As your personal representative, the broker

will perform all the necessary due diligence before alerting buyers of any properties that meet their criteria. For example, the broker will make sure that all parties are protected, that their best interests are being served and that he's not wasting anyone's time. As always, the broker will follow the Privacy Sale process and keep the buyer's identity, communications and intentions private. A Privacy Sale concludes when a buyer finds a home, then takes the steps to secure their new purchase in a trust (or a LLC owned by a trust) to further protect their financial interests and privacy.

In the end, it doesn't matter if you find a property that is on the open market or one that is off-market. The real value of working with well-connected brokers is in their ability to connect you with exclusive properties (some you would have never known about), their unique perspective on the area, their uncanny ability to point out a property's distinctive attributes and the not-so-obvious flaws, their negotiation skills, their deep understanding of the area's comparable property sales, their gut real-estate instincts and DNA, their "million-dollar Rolodex" of property service professionals, their unmatched remodeling and custom home building expertise, their ability to see opportunities or identify problems (before you even know they exist), their ability to keep you from making mistakes you don't even realize you're making, and their hyperfocus on providing you a red-carpet buying experience.

The bottom line is, having the right broker on your side gives you an unfair advantage.

If you're in the market to buy a property and would like to take advantage of exclusive off-market listings that are not available elsewhere, then I can help you get started. Just send me an email at Travis@PrivacySale.com, and we'll take it from there.

If you'd like to connect by phone, please visit www.privacysale.com/call to schedule a convenient time for an exploratory call with me.

"Are Privacy Sales for public figures only?"

Although Travis John Agency LLC believes that privacy concerns are arguably the greatest when you have reached public figure status, many other people benefit from our unique process. As you'll see, their reasons are not always privacy related. In essence, a Privacy Sale is a strategy that works in all instances when using traditional ways to sell a property are not the best (or preferred) choice.

Some people, including nonpublic figures, are drawn to this process due to their own privacy concerns, whatever they might be. Others use Privacy Sales to increase their safety and security. Public service employees, such as law enforcement officers, teachers, and firefighters, use this process to keep their home address out of the public eye, as do single mothers, the elderly, people who own homes in high-crime neighborhoods, and those who have nosy neighbors or have been through messy breakups.

Others use the process for convenience. For instance, they might be selling an investment property that is occupied by tenants or undergoing renovations. An active family might have limitations on when someone can view their home, so they use a Privacy Sale to limit the number of viewers. In fact, many people simply want the convenience of showing the home to prequalified buyers only.

People who have been through a financial hardship, such as a short sale, foreclosure, or a recent bankruptcy, often use the process because they seek discretion, and still others look to Privacy Sales as a solution to the time required and unpredictability of probate sales.

Other people see a Privacy Sale as simply involving less hassle.

And lastly, a Privacy Sale can often be the

best business decision because it allows an owner to avoid the dreaded "number of days on the market" and "price change" logs that are reported by the Multiple Listing Service (MLS).

Whatever the concerns may be, the Privacy Sale process is the same for public figures and nonpublic figures. It starts with a well-connected broker taking the time to understand the seller's very specific privacy and property sale goals; he or she then customizes a solution for the seller's unique needs.

As a matter of fact, many nonpublic figures are well served by using the MLS's own controls that can limit the exposure of their property.

Sellers can now decide to opt out or turn off some of the MLS's mass-marketing features. They can choose to go as far as hiding their property address from the Internet entirely, even from their own listing broker's website. Or, they can choose to have the property displayed on the Internet but to hide only the property address. Or, they can just withhold their property from specific websites, such as other participating broker's websites or syndicated and/or third-party advertising sites such as Zillow®. No matter what the seller decides, participating brokers and third parties must honor the seller's decision to opt out.

But the MLS's built-in features have obvious limitations. Every listing that is entered still becomes the property of the MLS and can be accessed by any of its participants for an indefinite period of time. So even with the MLS's highest restrictions in place, some sellers still believe that their property would be marketed too broadly and that they need more control over who knows and who doesn't know about their property sale.

There can be several reasons for this, including the fact that they can't control which MLS participants and brokers have access to their property information. And more important, there is no way to limit who the participants share their property information with, and how often the information is shared.

At the end of the day, a Privacy Sale is a bespoke marketing service.

Whether sellers crave privacy or less hassle, are trying to sell a property that has a tenant living there, or are in the middle of a messy divorce, they may find solace with the built-in MLS privacy and mass-marketing limiting features. For other nonpublic figures, a Privacy Sale may start with the seller opting out of MLS entirely. Maybe for some of the privacy reasons outlined in this book. Or, maybe because the seller is remodeling something at the property and doesn't want the number of days his or her property has been on the market for sale or any of the price changes recorded by the MLS. Whatever the seller's concerns are, a well-connected broker will help find the right-fit solution.

"COULD THE PUBLIC EVER FIND OUT ABOUT MY PRIVACY SALE?"

Yes, but this more often occurs when information is released by a seller's own staff, family members, vendors, employees, or friends. The intent of a Privacy Sale is to control the flow of information about your property, using ultimate discretion. Of course, at some point in the process, a prospective buyer will know your address. Although buyers are bound by mutual nondisclosure and confidentiality agreements, there is always a possibility that information about your privacy sale could become public knowledge. It bears noting that the number of people who could find out about your property sale is still very small compared to the number that could find out through traditional sale methods.

That said, a broker should always be focused on ways to keep information from being leaked to the public. Aside from the broker's own exhaustive measures to keep your information private, he or she should regularly advise all parties to pay close attention to this issue and limit the flow of information only to the parties directly involved in the Privacy Sale process.

"Is a Privacy Sale legal?"

Yes, a Privacy Sale is a legal way for sellers with privacy concerns to sell a property discreetly, and it is initiated only when the sellers prefer it.

Here are the guidelines a broker will follow for a Privacy Sale:

1. Inform the sellers of all options available to them and initiate a Privacy Sale only when a seller selects this as the best option. In most cases, the sellers provide written authorization not to place the home on the MLS and not to use any other traditional sale methods. A Privacy Sale is designed to benefit the seller only, not to serve the agent's interests.

2. A broker will comply with Fair Housing practices. Brokers are aware of their strict

legal and ethical duties not to engage in any type of unlawful discrimination. Laws prohibit discrimination in the sale, rental, or financing of dwellings and in other housing-related activities on the basis of race, color, religion, sex, disability, familial status, or national origin.

3. Brokers who communicate in a private group or portal will not mandate minimum commissions that must be paid to cooperating brokers, nor will they engage in any other price-fixing arrangements.

4. A broker will represent your best interests. The technical term in real estate is "agency relationship." In short, this relationship outlines how a broker represents your interests commensurate with his or her fiduciary duty. Agency relationships vary from state to state, and your broker will explain these relationships to you. Here's a brief explanation of the relationships:

In single agency, a broker represents only one party, either the seller or the buyer.

In dual agency, the listing broker represents both the seller and the buyer. A dual agent must not disclose confidential information to either party and must operate in a hands-off manner. Dual agency is not legal in all 50 states.

A transaction broker is a real estate agent who helps buyers, sellers, or both find common ground.

Florida law, for example, requires transaction brokers to provide services "honestly and fairly," exercising "skill, care, and diligence," and to disclose all known facts that are not readily observable to the buyer and which materially affect the value of a residential real property.

Disclosures are required only when brokers are representing clients in a "single agency" relationship, or if they are converting a single-agency relationship to a transaction brokerage relationship.

Selling real estate involves various statutes,

regulations, ethics rules and practical consid-erations. It is important to work with a trained and licensed broker who follows the right procedures to list, market, and sell your real estate.

CAN A PRIVACY SALE BE APPLIED TO OTHER LUXURY ITEMS?

Absolutely. The Privacy Sale process can be used to sell a yacht, a private jet, RV, an exotic car, or even a piece of artwork.

"I AM A WELL-CONNECTED BROKER. HOW CAN I USE THE PRIVACY SALE PROCESS IN MY BUSINESS?"

As a fellow broker, I know Privacy Sales are not possible, even fathomable, without well-connected brokers and the tight-knit net-works required to connect one-of-a-kind properties with one-of-a-kind buyers.

As you've learned in this book, my mission is

to help public figures and their families make better-informed real estate decisions. One of the ways I reach this goal is by providing a second-opinion service to buyers and sellers. Public figures and wealth holders already have a relationship with at least one broker, and usually with several brokers. So this service is just like getting a second opinion from their doctor, lawyer, financial planner, etc. It's my way of connecting Privacy Sale brokers with affluent sellers and buyers in their community. Through this second-opinion service, the seller or buyer will be able to quickly determine whether their level of service could be improved if they chose YOU to represent them.

The Privacy Sale network is for you if:

- You would like to share your off-market listings with other Privacy Sale brokers.
- You would like to know about off-market listings in your area.

- You would like to communicate with other like-minded pros.
- You would like to get high-quality referrals to wealth holders who are looking to sell or buy property.
- You would like to get access to the industry-transforming sales and marketing funnels, innovative tools, and private network needed to perform a Privacy Sale.

Personally, I love to geek out with other top brokers and find unique ways to help affluent sellers and buyers realize their real estate goals. For that reason, there are no costs or gotchas associated with being part of the network. BUT... you will need to meet certain criteria to be considered. Don't worry—it's nothing weird. It's just like the criteria you've read about in this book. Obviously, this is not for every broker—but for the right ones, it will be a perfect fit. The network becomes stronger only when the right people join, which is why you'll have to qualify to be part of the network.

How does it work? It's simple: this is just like your other cooperating broker relationships. If you receive a referral from Travis John Agency LLC and you are successful in helping the client sell or buy a property, then Travis John Agency receives a referral fee at the time of closing.

Your network is your net worth...

If you'd like to find out more about joining the network, just send me an email at Travis@PrivacySale.com, and we'll take it from there.

If you'd like to connect by phone, please visit www.privacysale.com/call to schedule a convenient time for an exploratory call with me.

ACKNOWLEDGEMENTS

As with all my endeavors, the first and most important acknowledgment goes to my wife and kids, who are the center of my universe and the source of all my passions. And who always forgive me for the times I am out—working on my craft.

Then there are my parents and step-father, Linda, Gary and Frank, who taught me basic manners and shaped me into a man who honors and respects privacy.

And all of my fellow entrepreneurs, extended family members and friends who gave me a strong support system as I worked on this book.

A special shout-out to the Genius Network

Mastermind Group's[1] Phillip Tirone, for connecting me with a great editor. And to Denise Gosnell, for the strategic legal counsel.

A huge extra thanks to my wife, Tonya, and to my editors, Jocelyn Baker and Proofread-NOW[2], who forced me to focus and relentlessly polish this book.

Finally, I want to acknowledge you, reader, for giving me your time and allowing me to share this new solution with you. I hope to hear from you soon.

1. www.geniusnetwork.com
2. www.proofreadnow.com

ABOUT THE
AUTHOR

TRAVIS'S STORY

A father, husband, perpetual traveler, minimalist, runner, health geek, adventure seeker, pioneer, street-smart entrepreneur and author, Travis has designed a life that allows him to stay sane, be present with his family and work with clients he loves.

Travis is the founder and chief strategist of Travis John Agency LLC. He is an innovator and well-known marketing and sales strategist who spends most of his time helping Already Successful™ business and luxury property owners get the most out of their assets.

For small-biz owners, entrepreneurs and busy professionals, Travis helps with strategic decisions, marketing direction and the innovation needed to ensure ongoing success. Simply put, Travis has a knack for finding unique ways to increase sales and solve top-shelf business problems.

For luxury property owners, Travis provides strategic advice and bespoke marketing solutions for real estate, yacht and RV sales. Travis accomplishes this using a unique blend of technology solutions, aggressive marketing strategies, and tight-knit social and professional networks.

Travis believes that the single best gift people can give the world is to bank on themselves. Travis is able to deliver his gift to the world by keeping his services simple, straightforward and focused.

Travis's entrepreneurial DNA became apparent in early childhood while he was doing everything from selling baseball cards and his parents' crap at the flea market to cutting his friends' hair in his garage and running a neighborhood lawn business. From there he has never looked back. Although he went off-course a few times, what remained constant was his ability to develop new ideas and see ways to put them to good use.

Other successful small-time ventures followed, but this pattern was one he would finally harness later in life. He is a late bloomer and an underdog, but he's got long-distance stamina (he won the mini marathon in 5th grade and later received a college scholarship for track and cross-country). Whatever Travis put his mind to, whether it was selling baseball cards or customizing his first car (Nissan Pulsar NX), he showed great potential at a young age. Without realizing it, he was creating the blueprint for his later successes.

After graduating from the University of North Florida with a bachelor's degree in health science, he cofounded Virtual Health, a preventive health services company that provided workplace solutions. He went on to work for one of the largest technology services companies in the world. As a sales manager there, he specialized in delivering IT solutions to Fortune 500 companies, generating tens of millions in revenue at a time for some of these companies. Working long hours, he made his employers rich, while his own health and spirit began to deteriorate.

Fast-forward five years—he was still working nonstop, this time in the distressed property market. As the founder of one of the first real estate short-sale agencies, Travis was quoted in publications such as *The Washington Post*, and he devoted most of his time to finding solutions for homeowners who had financial issues. Travis was fully immersed in the distressed property world, and he eliminated over $50 million in negative equity in Florida alone. At the same time, he founded a national referral network; a title and escrow agency; an advanced real estate sign installation business; and a real estate transaction service for attorneys, homeowners and real estate brokers to process paperwork and make routine bank calls. He then founded Short Sale My Yacht and became one of the first people in the country to apply real estate short-sale techniques to luxury items.

Although most people would have considered Travis successful (especially in the midst of the worst housing market ever) something was missing. Then it dawned on him—he had stumbled on the very thing that brought his success. It was MARKETING and his obsession with figuring out what actually drives business success. There was a direct correlation to his success and his passion to learn and implement the marketing and sales strategies that triggered exponential growth in his biz.

But Travis still struggled to connect the dots. In January 2010, when the world was still on the verge of an economic collapse, Travis and his wife, Tonya, had their third child. This event created a radical shift in Travis's mind-set and he really got clear on what life meant to him. Through this soul-searching, he realized his one-of-a-kind business experience and marketing know-how were extremely valuable—stuff that the RIGHT people would benefit from immensely. So that's exactly what Travis did. He narrowed the focus of his business to working ONLY with people he can be a hero to. Ultimately, he discovered his unique ability lies in his capacity to help affluent business and property owners get the most out of their assets.

Another big catalyst that pushed Travis to hyper-focus was his introduction to *The 4-Hour Workweek* by Tim Ferriss. This book opened his eyes to what he really was good at and what actually made him happy.

But more important, these life-altering events were a wake-up call for Travis. He has always created life on his own terms, but here was a reminder that he had fallen a little off-course. It was the kick in the pants that Travis needed to fine-tune his business around both his unique strengths and his lifestyle goals.

Travis has found that clients are attracted to working with him because of his natural ability to see opportunities before others do and then understand what it takes to nurture and develop these ideas—using his entrepreneurial instincts and marketing prowess to apply them.

Since falling in love with marketing, Travis has spent thousands and thousands of dollars on his own education, seeking out the best masterminds and mentors in the world. As a student of marketing, Travis is doing his best work when he's using his marketing muscles—whether it's finding unique ways to buy or sell multimillion-dollar real estate or identifying a new idea that doubles a business's revenue in 12 months. Travis now spends most of his time as an advisor to Already Successful people and their businesses.

AFFILIATIONS

Travis is a licensed, insured and bonded Real Estate Broker BK3100779, Yacht Broker YB7605 and Mortgage Loan Originator NMLS #374909 in the state of Florida.